# My Sister is Special

written by
## Larry Jansen

To Matthew, Nathan, and Andrew for being three of the best
brothers, or sons, anyone could have. To Rachel, for being the
one who consistently lights up our lives. And to Debbie,
for putting up with us all.

STANDARD
PUBLISHING
Cincinnati, Ohio

First Paperback Printing, 1998
© 1984, The Standard Publishing Company, Cincinnati, Ohio
A division of Standex International Corporation. Printed in U.S.A.
Library of Congress Catalog Card Number 97-47524
Catalog-in-Publication data available
ISBN 0-7847-0797-9

Hi. My name's Nathan. I like tacos, my hamster, and cartoons on Saturday morning. I don't like kissing on TV, Chinese food, or when my sister messes up my toys. But I like my sister. She's special.

This is my sister, Rachel. She likes being "mommy" to all her dolls, going to our brother Matthew's house, hugging, pretending she is a newscaster, and helping our younger brother, Andrew. She doesn't like walking barefoot on hot pavement, riding horses, or getting her face wet.

Each of us has different likes and dislikes because each person is special. God made us all special, so we are all different.

We are short or tall, skinny or not-so-skinny, old or young or in-between. God made my sister special, but in a different way.

Some kids are special because they are really smart. Some kids are special because they are really famous.

Some kids are special because they run fast or throw a ball far.

Some kids are special because they have physical problems and need wheelchairs or they are blind and need canes. My sister is special because she has Down syndrome. She learns slowly and needs special education.

I asked my dad how Rachel got Down syndrome. He said, "Your whole body is made up of tiny cells. Each of those cells is made up of chromosomes. You have forty-six chromosomes in each cell.

Twenty-three are from your father and twenty-three are from your mother. But your sister somehow got an extra chromosome, so she has Down syndrome."

This is what chromosomes look like under a magnifying glass.

It takes Rachel a long time to learn some things that I learn quickly, like eating and drinking, walking and running, thinking and talking. She can walk, but it took her a long time to learn how. She can talk, but not very well.

There are lots of people with disabilities.
Some people have Down syndrome,
like Rachel. Some people have other
kinds of disabilities.

Sometimes we stare at them, and maybe we don't know what to say or do when we see them. But we can be their friends. Don't make fun of them or their disability. Remember God made them, and they are special like you and me.

God wants us to be good helpers, but
I know there are lots of things people
with Down syndrome can do
for themselves.

If Rachel is having trouble I can ask her if she needs help, but sometimes the best help is to let her do it herself. Every kid needs the chance to do things on her own.

My sister is fun to play with. She wants to do the things I do, so I try to do good things. I can't imagine my family without Rachel.

I learn things from Rachel, too. She doesn't care
what people look like or where they live.
Rachel will be anyone's friend—
no matter what.

Mostly, Rachel teaches me about love. She shows me that God loves us all, no matter what.

I love my sister.
My sister is special!

# Advice for Parents and Teachers

I originally wrote this book to help explain Down syndrome to my children. Helping a child understand a peer with Down syndrome can lead to mutually beneficial friendships. Parents, teachers, or other adults in a child's life can encourage and facilitate special friendships using these suggestions.

1. Use the information on pages 10 and 11 to briefly explain Down syndrome. Tell your child that his Down syndrome friend's features—his slanted eyes, his short body, and his curved little fingers—are caused by his extra chromosome. Explain that his friend has feelings, likes, and dislikes just like he does.
2. Children with disabilities want to do things themselves as much as other children do. Encourage your child to let his friend be as independent as possible.
3. Make it easy for your child to include a friend with a disability in his social routine.
4. Children with mental retardation have speech delays. Teach your child to kindly ask his friend to repeat any words or phrases your child doesn't understand.
5. Encourage your child to introduce his friend with Down syndrome to some of his other friends. Express to your child that he and his other friends can learn things from his friend with Down syndrome, too.
6. Educate your child (and yourself) about the world of a child with a disability. Explain special education, therapy, medications, wheelchairs. Help your child to see these tools in a positive light—they are helpful to people.
7. Teach your child that God loves everyone, including his friend with Down syndrome. All of us are important to God. Jesus helped many people with disabilities. Help your child to share his faith with his friend with Down syndrome, and invite his friend to church.

Special thanks to Jim Pierson, director of the Christian Church Foundation for the Handicapped and consultant to Standard Publishing.